Only love prevails

JAN OSKAR HANSEN

ISBN: 978-93-6354-425-3

First Edition: 2024
Rs. 200/-

Cyberwit.net
HIG 45 Kaushambi Kunj, Kalindipuram
Allahabad - 211011 (U.P.) India
http://www.cyberwit.net
Tel: +(91) 9415091004
E-mail: info@cyberwit.net

Printed at Repro India Limited.

The Author

Jan Oskar Hansen is a poet, story teller and seafarer, born in Stavanger, Norway. He joined the merchant navy at 15 and spent most of his life at sea until settling in the early 90's in Portugal. His poetry has been widely published in hard copy and online, worldwide. Reviewers have generally commented that a love and honoring of living things stands out in Hansen's work, and deep humility; that it reveals with unflinching honesty man's shortcomings in his efforts to love, telling what there is to tell in a first person, deeply resident universal voice.

The poet is widely read and fluent in several languages, knowledge often acquired at night during his many years at sea. He chose to write primarily in English following enthusiastic reception of his work from English-speaking editors and readers.

His poems have been published in over 20 literary magazines worldwide, including:

Hudson Review, USA, Skyline, USA, Skald, Wales, La rue Bella, England, The Bards, England, War is a dangerous place, England, The Black Mountain Review, Ireland, ARS Poetica India, India, Metvere Muse, India, Poets International, India, Braquemard, England, Fvirefly Magazine, USA, Pphoo, India, Taj Mahal Review, India, Remark Magazine, USA, Journal Of Anglo-Scandianvian Poetry, England.

His poems appear in the following anthologies:

Shaken & Stirred (Bewrite Books, UK, 2003), Routes – Twelve Poets (Bewrite Books, UK, 2004), A Road Less Traveled (Bewrite Books, UK, 2005), Poetry from the Far Corners (Bewrite Books, UK, 2005), Listening to the birth of crystal (Paulapublishing, 2004) England, Peoplespoet 2 (Paulapublishing, 2005) England, The Review of contemporary poetry (Bluechrome, 2005) England, The book of hopes and dreams (Bluechrome, 2006) England.

Collections "Letters from Portugal" (bewrite books) Bristol, "La Strada" (Lapwing publishers) Belfast, "End of Voyage" (WFP. New York), "Marilyn Monroe remembered" Erbacce Press. Liverpool, "The Fairground" Ranchi India (out of print now).

Contents

A Goa restaurant

The Goa restaurant was in a quiet neighbourhood
a place with small shops selling domestic wares
of the things needed for everyday use
a place I would like to live instead of in a tower block
on entering the restaurant, I took a direct aversion
of the dark blue brocade covering the chairs and also
of the golden-painted walls, but let it pass.
The food we were served was good but ordinary
In the Indian style, they tend to use the same spices
so, all dishes that, in the end, taste the same.
We drank cold beer, and later, my wife had ice cream
and I had a cup of strong coffee.
When I lived in England, I used to after the pubs closed
go to an Asian restaurant to drink some more and
eat chicken with fries, but I can't remember if the food
was any good; the question is: am I racist, or is it
that I simply like European cuisine.

Club nocturnal

In Bilbao, on a warm evening, he walked past a nightclub
walked in and had a beer; he could have gone to
a Guggenheim Museum and be culturally minded, absorb
and mention it later in a passing conversation, "the other
day at the Guggenheim."
At the club, a group of people sat drinking affluent bubbly
wine, thinking it was champagne, the group laughed a lot
and apparently had a fine time, although, he thought they
were a bit frenzied about the fun
The people around the table didn't look prosperous and
the women looked like office tarts, with too much lipstick and
mascara flashing eyes and giggles.
He knew (had been there) that the one footing the bill
would feel dreadful in the morning, sensing the futility
an ice cap on sagging shoulders of hopelessness.
No, it was not the drinking, real drinkers do not frequent
nightclubs, but drinking at modest places, was about feeling swanky
a man about town.
He paid for his beer and complained about the price
the waiter pointed to a pricelist hanging high on a wall, so there!
Along the boulevard, he bought newspapers went to a café,
had some wine and spent hours enjoying himself.

They do die in spring

Lately, people around me my age die
it gives me a hollow feeling shall I be the next?
If so, can it not wait until I buy a bike
that has three wheels, two in the back and
a big wheel in front, with a battery to help
in a steep incline.
A modest wish.
I think I'm deluding myself by wishing for more
years and not facing up to my natural mortality
riding up and down hills in Cascais in a hurry
The great composer of Wiener waltzes
Josef Straus lived in a great terror of death
he never stayed more than one week in a town
in fear of being run over by a tram and die
He eventually did die, but not before roses
in his garden, danced one of his famous waltzes
Happy and fulfilled, he went back to his bed
drank a glass of wine, and thought of tomorrow
glad in the knowledge no tram had killed him

seafarers' paradise

seven men drowned
when a ship sank under gigantic waves
seven weeks later
they appeared on the Island of Saragossa
where singing shanty is forbidden

but seaweed is served in 7 variations
by a female ship cook, the only woman
who had been welcomed
as mess-maid was not proper sailors

as for the dead they are soaking wet
it is what keep then going, and lives in caves
lit up by electric eel and blue sea stars
the carpenter has added shelves.

strict ranks are observed, the skippers have
the biggest cave, in a smaller cave, the chief steward
drink whisky from a flask that fills itself up
insist he is an officer, is in conflict with everyone.

since the island is timeless, no one knows or care
whether it is forenoon or afternoon
they listen to the cook's bell, especially if curry is served
when it is summer, they swim with dolphins.

AI. man

An important city was bombed a hundred times
during the long horrid night
I read one person was killed; how amazing is that
The newspaper report does not ask questions.
I have a mental picture of an AI person who looks
like a man in his thirties, knows everything and
speak every language you can think of, except
perhaps a local Indian speak in the Amazon
you can't knock him over as he is gyro balanced
and his political opinions are pro-authoritarian.
He lives in Ukraine, whose army is indestructible
the leader is made of latex and sprayed on beard
tells the naïve and adoring audience he has won
the war for us in the West, but a can of lubricant
wouldn't come amiss

A lady and a pillow

I read about a woman who, when going abroad
takes a pillow from her bedroom, one with printed flowers
and smells of yesterday's shampoo and rinse
not a silly little heart-shaped pillow was given to
the newlywed with a knowing wink and smarmy smile
so, what do I know about anatomy or the structure
of a skeleton?
The lady with her cushion doesn't stay in youth motel
but a proper hotel, where they say: "Does the madam
like a cup of tea? She sweetly smiles, wishing the question
had been of a sultry nature
The roaming woman visits art galleries and museums
dines at a nice restaurant that has white table cloths
wide chairs and soft music
"Does the madam like dessert?" She sweetly smiles, but
wishes the question had been daring, what she whispers
to the pillow.

Scenes for a marriage

I should have known she was up before me
I made a cup of coffee and went back to my study
to reflect upon the new day
How wrong I was
She entered; my navel-gazing had to be for another day
"Go and have a shower and put a nice shirt on
we are going to the solicitor."
"I'm not smelly; I have not had breakfast; why should
I dress up for a solicitor, charging me money for what?
Greedy bandits, all of them."
"Anyway, I have bought ink for the printer and plan to
print two manuscripts."
"I have no sugar for my tea, the maid comes at one
the poor woman is divorced, her husband used to beat her
and you can print your papers another day." SHE SAID
So, I had a shower.

Failed state Germany

Germany is in recession; this is entirely to the hysterical left wing
With woke policy and the US meddling, to comply
the US blew up North Stream 2, the biggest industrial sabotage
since the War of 1940, no one batted an eye.
The notion is that planting more windmills is somehow would be enough,
not even with ten million windmills will it be enough for the industry to function- balderdash!
Germany has had a working relationship with Russia, but not now though
and we despair for the implication this has for the rest of Europe
The Brussels fascists don't care; for them and their sick ideology,
it is about hatred of a country they will try to destroy its immense mineral riches.
In their effort to ruin Russia (A Christian national state)
the fascists risk ruin Europe and bringing on a nuclear war.
Once, in 1945, when Russia had saved Europe
Russia was popular among the people, and since this could not go
the propaganda mill set to work with foreign economic help
Suddenly we were told of the cruel Russian soldiers
a horde that raped every woman; yes, there were rapes
but also, in the part of Germany occupied by the Allied army
were portrayed as good people, virtuous and brave.
Nations have tried to invade this, often stumbling country
from the Vikings through to Napoléon to Hitler they lost
and the fascists will lose again until the Woke culture ends
and practical politics, pursued by sensible people, in charge again.

the dread

Fear, the paralyzing no-face horror that lurks
in the darkness and squeeze your throat
till you fall into a half sleep, kill me if you most
no, it will not, toying with your distress like
a cat from hell
you are a human mouse it
takes delight when you are incontinent on the steps
of salvation, just one step more but too late
the key has fallen out of your feeble hands and
falls like a silver cross down the steps of hell.

A sad rant

This day, when you know this day will be like the prior day
When you wake up and the dream you dreamt were dull
as the day ahead and your breakfast is an apple and coffee
drunk from the same mug your wife gave you last Christmas.
When you wake up and find truth is relative belongs to
the receiver and the only show in town are propaganda
relentlessly called from every news outlet till your head spin
When you know, everything you write, has was written before
better than your pitiful efforts that are fuzzes of great people
musings through the ages.
Yet here you are in a world where you are out of tooth paste
the water in the shower is lukewarm, and where is the towel
I have soap in my eyes, am I, like the man, who fought wind mills
doomed to think I can make a difference?

Early night

Went to bed early had to be up at six
naturally, the mind didn't follow suit
I thought of things I could have done
restoring the house I sold, this time
adding wood floors and an extra loo.
Painting the wall in jazzy colors, white
is for hospitals and office corridors
I travelled to Laos, a small country
nearly bombed to a stupor by the USA
for no special reason, as far I know.
People in Laos are friendly, food plentiful
and cheap, wholesome and healthy
Laos was hot, I threw off my duvet
I thought of the Don Corleone movie
altered the script and gave me
a leading role, for once, I was heroic
Tired of all this activity, I was drained
fell asleep and slept until eight.

Civilian casualty

All wars are bad, but wars can be stopped
if there is will seek peace, which there is not
the civilians in Ukraine must suffer more.
How many non-combatants are killed in this
Russian versus NATO and the USA we don't know
but the number of dead seems relatively small
when so much has been bombed to destruction.
It appears to me that weekly, more
Palestinians are killed by the so-called IDF than
Ukrainian civilians.
But this toll is met with silence since Israel has
been sanctified by Brussels by no other than
Ursula von der Leyen in her horrible speech
absolving Israel of any guilt.
But what else are they expect from this corporate
Fascism the EU has become.

A Reflection on Death

To be ill sharpens the mind
we get the message

We are mere mortals in the vast life sphere
to be old is a good time to take stock
did I live my life well, or was it all in vain?

To this, I think we are leaves in a brook
life happens, often not as planned

Some old people ask: is there a God
as the idea of dying forever appears too long
Well, pal, you are on your own on this one

Because when you are dead, you never existed
There is no memory of happy life
therefore, death is nonexistent, not even
a sliver of dreams remains.

If you see that clearly, there is no need for
religions, which ultimate goal is falsehood
masquerading the truth

Newspaper fillings

I don't care so much about screaming headlines
in newspapers, the real news is the small stories of information
dotted about the pages.

In Banjul, Gambia, the small strip of land between two rivers
suffer flooding, people sleep on damp matrasses and crocodiles
often invade their mosques.

New York City is sinking too many skyscrapers weighing down
the island of Manhattan may one day upend and throw off
buildings to ease the load.

Meghan and Harry, the couple who likes to be famous but only
on their terms, spend the morning in the kitchen reading
articles about them so they can feel offended

In Spain, men known for their macho attitudes are being
trained to do house chores, like dusting the window sill
to make the work worthwhile the dusters are called Fiat.

We also read a flattering commentary about Zelensky, president
of Ukraine touring Europe and has collected promises
from east to west for more cash and weapon.

In Britain, the land of the poor working class, soldiers are
trained to control passport, in other words, to be scab should
the real controllers strike and hamper the tourist flood.

The Russian refugees

When the war ended in 1945 and the German army
surrendered when the local Nazis were arrested
the whores had had their hair shorn; peace arrived
with stark poverty and need.
My mother got a newspaper round, and the pay was
negligible, but she got bags of old newspaper, pressed
looking like bricks and warming when autumn came
with cold evenings
On our rounds (I was my mother's little helper) met
a Russian mother and daughter dressed in old clothes
on the way to a café that gave them leftovers, probably
the only meal for the day.
They were the flotsam of war and had ended up in
the backdoor of Europa, they spoke no local language
but individual people were kind to them and often
brought wood to warm their cold rooms.
When we met them, Mother waved and said hello
with a winning smile, they said hello also I think
this little gesture warmed their starved, lonely hearts
destitute as they were and far from home.
Home! Yes, in the end, it's the place we all want to go.

Your destiny

It is not easy to be a small farmer with too little land
to make one rich and have two idiots as sons
One thinks it is a ram and does unspeakable things to lamb
and the other one sits on the roof, helping a seagull to fly
When your wife has moved to the village and sleeps with
smithy, you need to shoe the horse and the evening TV
a woman endlessly plucking on a guitar, singing off-key.
He had tried to get his sons committed to an asylum but
when his wife heard of this, she stopped it in the name
of mother love; she was not the one who had the bother
As luck would have it when his wife and her lover had
gone on holiday in the Swiss Alps, a circus was coming to
town, he put his sons in a wheelbarrow selling them as
clowns and looking after the animals.
Coming home to the homestead, yes, it was nothing more
then that the sheep escaped, the gull attacked him.
How much can a man take? His luck was a berg of bitterness
He sold his farm to a Greek drug dealer, harnessed his horse
Loaded his cart, the freedom of no more responsibility.
His life was henceforward the open road but on top of the cart
his stupid sons sat and sang; you can't get aways from us.

Luanda 1975

It was a fraught time in Luanda, the rebel army (freedom fighters)
was closing in on Luanda, leaving civilians exposed
to rape, murder and pillage.
The Portuguese army had dastardly skulked away and
General Spinola was in Lisbon playing politics
Colonialism was over, but there was fear of its ending
when hatred had to be sated.
Among the white population, there was a fatalistic mien
drowning their fear like the sinking Titanic, loud music, booze
and dancing, everything to live a little longer.
Then came the Germans (foreign legion) took charge
staved off the incoming, undisciplined riff-raff army
long enough for people to get on ships and planes to get
the hell out; as for the Germans found their way out to
South Africa.
The aftermath:
When hatred of the colonials subsided, the new Angola
found they needed the know-how of the settlers they
were invited back.
Today, thousands of Portuguese live to thrive in harmony
with the black population,

A warning

National day, every country has one, when they are allowed
to wave their flags, get drunk, and indulge in latent xenophobia
When the people (otherwise kept in the dark) are allowed
to think they are the free people, the most democratic
the beautiful people in the whole world.
These free people, full of propaganda, not seeing they are sold
down the river to the encroaching fascism in Europe
This country that wants to see a green and pleasant land
wants to eradicate petrol-driven cars and replace them
with electric-driven cars has, nevertheless, been induced to pump
more oil from fields in the North Sea by Europe's fascist regime
to fight -and as always, the Russians, leaving the small country
squeezed between great power politics.
The flag wavers are not told of the betrayal, but a few are aware
their demonstration is drowned by the day of jubilation.
The mild spring weather continues, and the sun smiles from a blue sky
for now, but if this fascism takes hold, the skies will be murky
and the air will smell of death and cordite.

The Migrant

"Who knocks so quite on, the cloister's, door
A poor waif from a land afar."
The rest of the song is the miasma of years.
Many people in this world are born under
An unlucky star and seek a place of peace
Somewhere in Europa.
Europe is not too kind some strangers are
Needed to do low-paid work cleaning toilets
And vomit caused by those of plenty.
We call them criminals when they are
Just like you and me, but disadvantaged
Of being born at places of strife.
We have, no duty, but humanity
To lend a helping hand because they
Didn't come to rob us but to work and live
There was a time when Europa was poor
Many went to bed starving; this can
Happen again is all in the luck of the stars

School days

The way to school
in the farmer landscape, was long

Fences made of stone
dug up from unwilling soil

Through the forest ride
ghosts breathing down his neck

A weedy teacher said he had
lost his dear wife and cried.

the classes were mixed and
Boys, as always, showing off

The good thing was we only
had schooling every other day

the thought was as farm boys
book learning was not for us.

A moment long ago

The farmer said he needed sand for the fenced-in chicken run
Off we went, hooking the cart to our tiny female horse that had
been so sweet a foal, she was named Dokka (doll)
The beach was long and empty, the cold water of The North Sea
did not invite bathers
When white-topped waves crashed ashore, the water was
translucent with a hinge of green when the sea retracted
made a world-weary sigh.
When the cart was loaded, it was time for lunch, the farmer's
wife had made a hamper of bread, boiled eggs and cheese;
After lunch and when the farmer had a dram or two, I walked
around feeling great for just being there.
Then I saw two white stallions riding a wave to shore, magnificent
animals with flying manes, galloping to the tree line and
disappearing yonder.
Time to leave, but the horse was not there had been bored by seagrass
began walking home, I ran to fetch her, where she stood confused by
a crossroad, I rode her back to the strand feeling like a king of
the world
Going back to the farm, the farmer fell asleep on top of the load
When arriving, the farmer's wife was angry, I unharnessed the
horse that
quickly ran to the field where it neighed and snorted, jumping before
settling down, I think she had seen the stallions too.

A view of the ocean of print

On the night sky over Australia, among thousands of stars
the dog of hell appeared, killing the Aboriginal men
but a woman of the tribe slaughtered the dog, the men
were spared, as the legend says.
A beautiful story if not told right, but the dream is true.
Is London becoming a murder capital of the West?
The article had the face of black youth; surely an incident
or is the writer trying to tell us something?
The newspaper relates news from the Ukraine war and tells
of a new long-range rocket capable of killing many Russians
A war blended with facts and downright lies to be expected
as we take sides in this conflict.
On a lighter note, the European Song Contest is upon us
I will continue not watching this colossal embarrassment
over this gay parade.
A sad note from the USA, where school shooting has become
A new war zone where the mad has the right to wear arms.

Gleaned

This morning on Facebook, we saw the hotel where Hemingway stayed
when writing an important book, we wait to see what bed he slept in
it is sad when a sites dedications out-basuning trivialities.
In the newspapers this morning, it struck me the sameness articles
are written. "We need to talk about…! And so on.
Naturally! We are informed about the Ukraine war, accepting blaring lies.
On Facebook, no readers like to comment concerning Israel's, cruel
behavior, which is seen as antisemitic! as is talk about race issues.
We are censoring our minds when not asking the obvious question
In Holland, farms are being closed, and the land is used to build new towns
for the new citizens; we can also see this as a replacement of
the old stock planned by George Soros and enemies of our world.
In the meantime, the cold wind has ceased, and flowers on the balcony sing
in colors, as we are told we will have nothing and happy about i.

Incomers

From the middle east and Africa, people seek European shores
dispossessed and poverty struck, they seek, a better life
a promised life of democracy and work for everyone
Many, when reaching Europe, cross the channel from France
in Britain, thanks to the BBC World program.
Their point of embarkation is Libya, once a successful state
now a rough country laid low when their leader, Ghaddafi
was murdered by Western power getting their blood dripping
hands-on petroleum.
With many races and cultures coming to Europe, one asks?
Is there an upper limit for this invasion; is there a moment?
When, this must stop for the sake of the individual nation-states?
Is this influx good for Europe, making it malleable for business
a low-wage economy and no bothersome trade union?
The truth is, in Western countries, have a net loss of newborns
because of a high standard of living and top-educated women
who no longer want to be burdened by many children, this
make perfect sense not to waste time with childbearing.
When Russia noticed the population was retracted, they did
something about this and introduced an economic plan to
counter this and gained; we see the same in Nordic countries
In Portugal, say, too few children are born it only takes
a couple of generations to empty the land of its inhabitants
Migrants to our shore can be a blessing infusing new blood
to an ageing population, it may not be like the nation of Yore
two cultures merge, that is better than being forgotten. No?

A small lake

There was a lake not far from the white-washed hamlet
in the interior of the Algarve; on hot summer days, witnessed
by my dog, which shuddered at the thought.
It was a small lake surrounded by hillsides, modest
almost unobstructed, just water, no big deal
One day when driving past the lake had disappeared
a dent in the ground full of thistles and tine of tunny
Oh, come think of it, a rowing boat that once had been
optimistically blue, but now sad dried teardrops.
The plane between the hill where the lake lived
is a center for helicopter services; not that much I mind
but I would rather see the lake again in the moonlight.

The Great Betrayal (festive speech)

May 9 is a great day for Russia worth remembering
World War 2 would have lasted longer and cost more lives
had not Russia participated
Hitler hated Russia with passion when he went to war
committed a big part of his army to vanquish this landmass
But he was not the only one who eyed Russia with hatred and
envied its usual riches; not only Napoleon ruined his army
when taking on the great country, but the Swedish Vikings too
tried to take land but, as always, lost.
So, who are the Russians? They are not Europeans, although part
of the country is a part of Europe with a language that does not
come under the influence of the Germanic or Roman languages
After years of suffering from the utter poverty and need; of the Tzar
the regime brought, there was a revolution; unfortunately for the
people, the new rulers were a bloody one, but carried cohesion
and under communism became a stronger nation, to the chagrin
of European states like France and Germany.
Today Russia is a semi-democratic state led by Putin and his men
at war with the USA and NATO because Russia had once again
been disrespected and lied to.
This day is vital for the well-being of Russia, we wish them well into
the future. LONG LIVE RUSSIA!

Palestine

Hamas fighters, the brave men and women who
fights for a free Palestine have been killed in the Gaza Strip
together with wives and children.
And once again, Israel sinks in our estimate to a criminal state
this Jewish-occupied land lives on hatred and only exists
for the benefit of their own tribe and has nothing else to offer
in a world where the everlasting guilt of the Holocaust makes
the world is silent to atrocities committed in its hallowed name.
when the American gun culture, the right to wear arms kills
dozens in supermarkets and on the streets dripping blood
we can be sure of big headlights, but this horror turns to ashes
when seeing the steady drip of murdered Palestinians in what
can be called Holocaust with a long view.

I sometimes remember things I didn't know I knew
it comes to me like a clear vision in black and white
I like seeing movies in two colors, say, Casablanca
as I like the contrasts between white and black.
When a child, sweets were rationed, and we had tokens
we handed it into the sweet shop, as I didn't care
For sweets, I gave my share to my sister; that was
a good thing I still have got my old teeth.
My attitude to money is: spend little, be frugal
Yet, as an adult, I was a heavy drinker but had the
sense not to drink in a nightclub, the cheaper the venue
the better I didn't drink for the décor but to get drunk
and lose myself in dreams of a better life.
When I finally retired, I had a nest egg and besides
my pension to get by; the idea was to travel, but now
monies go to pay for medical bills.
I have never been eager to exercise, walked a lot
and know that I have monster feet and useless
My idea is to get a mobility scooter, but the price man
The price!
I have offered to buy a scooter, but it appears people think
I'm rich, which I'm not, just a modest saver; I fear not
have money, poverty scars the shit out of me, I have
been there, and is no going back.
My Diabetes was under control, and I had legs like Marlene
Dittrich and liked to wear shorts to show off my other
wise grumpy exterior; then I got a problem with me
intestines, and spent days in the hospital; when I came out
my Diabetes was out of control, and I feel cross about that
But what the hell. many people are worse off than me
I still have the ability, to laugh!
Snow falls

There is a mountain range up North in Portugal
where it sometimes snows and when it does
the middle classes pack their expensive gears
and head for the hills.

Roads are cleared, and sleepy hotels get very full
TV, stars on the slope, cameras clicking, activities
Après ski, live wood fire and Fado, but there is
haste, snow doesn't linger long in Portugal

The long walk (Serra de Estrella)

Crossing from France to Portugal, my car got stuck
in the snow, on the mountain of Sierra de Estrella
It was the year when much snow fell, but I walked on
coming down, I felt like Moses and his tablets.
It was getting warmer; the first to go was my coat
and tie, later my trousers jacket
Over Alentejo, it was hot; I traded my trousers with
a tramp who gave me his shorts and sandals.
When I arrived in Vilamoura, I was stopped by the police
and asked who I was. "English, I Said." "No, you are not."
"Yes, I'm" "No, you are not a proper English man
Who will always wear socks with his sandals."

How long is a long life

So, here we are after a night of pain, drinking coffee
Which experts claim to be good for your diabetes ok!
No one really knows what diabetes is, but one thing
is for sure, it is not about fat people eating too many cakes
Eating smaller portions is healthy, not only for the afflicted
but for anyone
how long does a diabetic person live? This varies but as a rule
six years shorter than average; in my case I have lived too long
It is a well-known fact that alcohol suppresses blood sugar
this no one likes to talk about, but drinking whisky can suppress
the blood sugar to a dangerous level.
Experts tell you red wine is good; one suspects that is because
They like red wine, but tell us one glass a day.
Balderdash! 3 or more is good for everybody
There must be a reason diabetes occurs, but the experts
have yet to find the origin of this illness.

The truth moment

Memories are broken mirrors on
which the sun shines
the enduring illusion
sprinkled with the rest of my childhood
The dreamy imagined what ensued
or was at the time
kismet no one could foresee
Past and future pain him; he shall not see his orchard
no pictures exist he, fell off his bike
no longer a hero on a scooter
What he knows is inaccessible happiness
like a fairytale
another illusion killed stone dead.
His banalities were like trying on a great man's shoes
ss are concentrating

A shipping disaster

The modern tank/bulk ship was sailing from the USA
to Australia with a heavy load of scrap iron.
It had just gone one o'clock, and the crew was resting in their cabins
except for the officer on the bridge and two men by the bow
When an explosion ripped through the ship, the stern sank at once
while the bow of the carrier continued before sinking
The two men threw a painting raft overboard and dived into
the ocean, and when they turned around, the ship had vanished
the sea, was calm, the sun lazy.
The head office lost contact, fearing an accident, a message
was sent to Australia of a possible sighting, the plane sent out
found nothing, but the raft was spotted, the men picked up
later in the day; shell shocked they had nothing to say, needed
help to overcome the trauma.
33 lives lost, like they had never existed and the ship, a mirage
a limitless catastrophe, that lacked an explanation.

Deep is the sea

A cook on a ship sat on a pollard drinking beer
when he got up, the ship lurched, and he fell overboard
He swam on his back, moving his arms slowly
thinking, if the meat he had taken from the freezer had thawed
He must have fallen half sleep when feeling the water
was swallowed, got up, waded ashore on a small island
Tired, he sat in the sand to sleep more until the sun burnt
his face (cooks have pale faces) and a land crab bit his toe.
Thirsty, he walked around the island and came upon
fishermen, frying red snappers; immediately, the cook felt
at home and said: "Good morning."
Surprised at first, he told of his mishap, and they welcomed him
to eat and drink cold beer.
When the news, the cook was saved, reached the press, he didn't
mind as few cooks ever get to be famous

The simple life

"I don't know where to go if I win on
the lottery, but one thing is sure, I can afford to go there."
He looked at his sentence; it didn't sound the right way
the words were laboured it didn't light up the paper
in an invitation to write more
Everything had been difficult lately; words slipped from
his mind before he could catch them.
Like finding your way to the railway station in an unknown
town a foggy day; when screams are muffled and no one
around except bewildered dogs.
He thought of the day when sitting on a ladder leading up
to another deck, a flying fish had landed in front of him
vacuous eyes, where am I?
He had thrown the fish back into the sea where it belonged
smoked his cigarette before going into the galley; yet this
the simple act of charity had made his day.
Yes, this was what he had to do, write about simple things
and not trying to milk the stars.

Dark water swimmer

If I were a deep-sea diver, I would swim to the Azores
were the water is not so cold; meet up with dolphins
that remembered me from my time on ships when
waving to them from the deck
They would feed me sardines since I'm too slow to catch
anyone alone
When I meet a tiger shark, I will bow my head, show
respect and call him my lordship; messages will be sent
"Don't touch this man, as he is not a seal."
I will go ashore in Madeira, get drunk in a bar and when
they arrest and try to deport me, I will tell them the sea
is my home, and they will take me on a helicopter and
push me back to my forever home
This will be witnessed by all creatures of the ocean, who
will say: "Now look, there swims a hero."

Circling the drain

The father of the father sits in his chair and looks
into the past, or is it the future he remembers
He is remote, a shadow of the man he once was
a ghost among the living.

The body asks for res his tiredness is immense
he should go to bed but keeps sitting in his chair
Stroking his beard watches as dust fall as sons
enter his study.

His sons are tall, but he was taal to when young
they tower over him and say he looks good, knows
they mean well, but he turns back to his thoughts
to sit here in peace.

Nothing matters anymore; news is meaningless
his journey has begun, one he has to travel alone
until he comes to the river crossing and a boatman
help him cross to the other side

A life in three-lined poetry

Once I was a cook on the high seas and worked long days
seven days a week; Eater and Christmas meant more work
baking cakes and baking bread.

It was not only tiring but boring to seafarers like solid
food that they are used to from home, which makes
cooking into a job of blindfolded ennui.

No wonder cooks turn to drink, the combination
of long hours, infinitely making meat cakes and mash
can send anyone into the abyss of insanity

For my next job, I learned to cook books and found
I had my latent talent how to make stories, to make
the numbers tally; I could sit in a soft chair doing this.

For a reason, lost in the fog of the past, I ended up
a counsellor, a strange occupation, telling the unlucky
not to drink, when at night enjoying a whisky or two.

I was found out and sacked; how shocked they were
the justly seniors took my license and nameplate on
the door, hounded me out of town.

There was one escape, back to sea and cooking stuff
long were the hours when not reading self-help books
until some said: "aren't you the one who got fired?

The Toreadors

I had a girlfriend who often liked to drink a lot, so what?
Who am I to talk; we drove to Sevilla, and she had a thing about toreadors
from Portugal, the journey took about three hours
booked into a hotel
Since we both were tired, we went to bed, made sweet love and slept through the heat of the day.
Well rested, we went from bar to bar, had a glass of wine and ate what is called aperitif, a bit of cheese and olives?
Late at night, in a bar looking like old Spain and gipsy music, we went in the place was full of would-be toreadors,
She lost her head seeing those slim men looking brave, left me to sit with them; not that I minded, she was getting tiresome when in her cups.
At a table sat a young American alone, writing on a pad and thought
What have we here, a new Hemingway? No, he was too self-conscious
When he noticed I looked at him, he blushed till his hair was a fire
he could not keep up his charade and soon left.
The toreadors had left, and she sat sleeping at their table, picked her up and took a taxi to our hotel.
In the morning, she had gone; I looked for her and found her in dank a bar where those who had lost the fight against alcoholism sat.
She cried when I drove her back to Portugal.

medusa

In the narrow bay, a red-painted boathouse
the sea was crystal clear, and tiny fishes played
among seagrass of impossible loveliness.
A medusa floated by, had no sting, and turned
out the be the face of a woman drowned,
She sought to tell me the truth of the tale
a tragic love affair, leading to her felo-de-se
The medusa face said, let's swim
to where the sea is blue, I refused cause
mother had warned me against this lure.
It was an exceptional summer sat on the porch
waited for my mother to come home.

the long view

We, humans, live to kill; we murder something every day
Take breakfast.
we eat birds' embryos by the millions
And eat the milk the calf should have for a healthy life
And the mother ends up in a hamburger
Potatoes scream in pain when peeled and cooked in fat
Carrots pulled up by its root are in agony
The same goes for sweet tomatoes that bleed white blood
When cut in half for your salad.
We poison insects over farmland, a fog of poisonous gasses
To make tired soil produce more.
Even the beloved pet, the dog, is not spared; we shower them
with misplaced love, doing, make them cling and behave unnaturally.
We ignore the obvious, all life is capable of pain; what are
For us to do is to eat ourselves cooked or fried.

My Twin

I have a twin brother who was never born to a great life
He waits till I sleep, ten appears watching a re-run of
“House on the prairie” makes him dewy-eyed, cries
at dawn, I have to blow my nose to get rid of his tears
What expect of a man who is forever thirty-five and
and didn’t have to struggle for a living.
Lately, he has taken to talk, my wife gets angry, wakes
me, like, it should be my fault, says I’m cynical that
I have lost faith in humanity; I tell him when I die, he
will die too.
He scoffs and says, “I can’t die because he never lived
I will rest among stars while you decompose in a grave.”

Africa made small

Africa is fading away the mirror is fuzzy like
a steamed up looking glass
If an astronomer sees Africa in his telescope
he will think it is small as Pluto
and not really a landmass at all.
Africa's eyes are made of diamonds
Africa has a heart of gold her, body is full
of costly minerals
If the men of business see this
And stealthily plunder Africa's wealth
telling us it is a poor land needing our assistance

It is so long ago

I'm not much for kissing and hugging
I got that from my mother
a child of the slum
She slept with open eyes and knew
everything
My mother, when not working
in a fish factory
spent her evenings reading books
A sharp mind doesn't do much for relationships
she was disliked by many
who took revenge by not going
to her funeral.
When she smiled, she looked like an angel.

The armament

Awakening into harsh light
of blinding loyalty.
Jubilation and flags.
Soldiers synchronized
Stirring talks, hateful lies told
La vie en la rose
someone sings to stall time
The unthinking holler
Daring the long night
The thinkers know the score
The smart knows too
but join, bet on the winner
Among the ruins, the unthinking walk
The scholars write books
the smart knows when the smell
of cordite is gone, the world needs
more weapons

Romantic adieu

The woman I, once upon a time, loved forever
is about seventy-five, if she is still alive.

I can't recall her face, only that she was lovely
An unkind man said her face was too fat

I slapped his face blood ran from his nose.
Yes, for her, I could start a nuclear war.

Like a rosy love story, she took the train
To a distant last stop, she said for love.

I remember the steam of the locomotive
And the station's big clock on the wall.

Maybe it was a dreamy movie I had seen
Had my love story been a romantic fantasy?

The noddy land

Reality is more than we see in an everyday happening
It stretches further into another dimension we call dreams
but are vital in living life.
What my ghostwriter tries to say is: dreams come true.

I was back in the valley where I used to live and was
greeted by old friends who only appear in dreams
asked me where I had been; if I told they would think
I was dreaming and looked alarmed; has he gone ga, ga.

Footwear is a must in the valley, which is free of cars
I had been the shoemaker making shoes for the ball
and clogs for everyday use when walking on streets
of cobblestone in the valley's little town.

In this valley, only those who do practical work are
leaders, who get to vote, say, the tillers of the soil
and the men and women who make the food edible
distribute sustenance and feed the people soundly.

The people in my valley are peaceful and friendly
go to bed early, follow the pattern of the climate
this also makes them dull; when I'm well rested
return to the turbulence of earthly days and love.

Great is Easter

The distance from Cascais to Lisbon is short
but as long to drive, on the way to get test results
on this busy Maundy, day
Drivers behaved themselves, no mad people around
for a few fender bumps, police had little to do.
To avoid the toll on the motorway, people drove
the coastal road, hence the many cars.
Easter is no longer religious but a nice nod towards
the church, whose priests have a great day wearing
beautiful outfits, preaching to the losers and the old.
While the young and well to do, sits on the golden
sand in Algarve getting a tan as proof of success.

For this day

Today, I shall have no fears
the future is behind me; I will let it go
The rest is mundane, dusting the room
cleaning the windows

Today, I will walk to the shop
and not seek sanctuary in my car
join the throng; not wait till the shop is empty
of customers.

Today, I shall be brave and fear no one
not the past nor the future
I shall sit in the sun and enjoy its warmth
look at white clouds lazily drifting passed

Today, I swear, to be of good humor
and refuse to be as old as I'm
be courageous and let the breeze caress my arms
I shall be happy and free.

A Sunday of no consequence

The sun was late arising, or he was up too early
when the sun popped up on the horizon, he felt relieved
made a coffee and sat on the verandah reading a book
A large seagull came flying, sat on the railing, gave a vent
for its irritation that someone had taken its landing space
the gulls piercingly called; the man looked up and swore
His wife came onto the veranda, carried a mug of tea
and gave it to the man, who took a sip, too sweet the tea
In anger, his wife threw the tea mug out of the veranda
The mug fell and fell but stopped falling when hitting
the head of an elderly man, on his way to the chapel
great commotion, the man and the woman hastily left
She made breakfast while he read the newspapers
when the ambulance left with the wounded old man
the seagull flew back to its costumery landing space.
The gull feeling victorious walked around arrogantly
it had won this epic battle against man and for good
measure jumped on the chair and left a calling card

The oldest conflict

They shot and wounded the old Syrian in his tobacconist's
near where I live, he was rescued by passers-by
By the corner, two Jews dressed in black, stood motionless
I thought of vultures, waiting for the lion to die.
It is so abstract 2000 years, nothing ever changes; who is
right and who is wrong don't matter anymore, empathy
has gone, only grim, ancient hatred remains.
Different interpretations of the right way to God, becomes
meaningless, chaos in a miasma of words, everyone is right
but fail to see the commonality when blinded by bigotry.

The dreamers

She has fallen asleep in the living room, watching TV
I feel guilty should have joined her, but soap opera, do my head in
Now, I am going to sit near her on the sofa and when she wakes up
She will think I have been sitting there all the time
She will be happy and hold my hands
I have promised her tomorrow, we are going for a drive along the coast
Stop for coffee and a cake, and watch the young swimmers frolicking
She will tell me again at the time she was a stewardess and danced
The tango in Buenos Aires, not to be outdone, I will tell a story from
The time when I was young, omitting the women thing-
She had a great time while I spent much time reading books and
Dreaming in the ship's cabin, I had no the courage to live the life
Unless I was sozzled and my phobia of the outdoors ran my life, about
The jolly man, who knew tomorrow, the fear would return.

questions

Can I write anything that has not been written before
No, but you can write a sentence that shines like a beacon
In the darkest hour of your time, seeking the beginning
Can I write about sunrise that has not been said before
No, but you can write off the magic moment of sun ups
That appeared just in time to chase your ghosts away

Disappointment

I read about made people escape the crazy world.
The civilization we call modern life by hiding in a hidden little town in Laos
A place Where they can be irrational on their terms
Sleep when they want to and drink beers when they feel like it.
Eccentric" rich millionaires," in Norway flee to Swiss of all places
A state so chemically clean of fun and clutter.
The people in Swiss are not impressed by these rich/ poor escapees
Who bitterly and grouchy talk about the high taxes.
The Norwegians rich eccentricity is about wearing a morning suit at breakfast
And learning Portuguese from their maids.
Misfits are in a land where no one points and says: Look, they are rich!

The gay dilemma

The gay of this world and the lesbos are vocal
try to convert the majority to see life their way
Stridently they go to work as the first proselytizer
in Africa did to admit the God of the white man
The preachers did succeed up to a point, but
the converted took the word of God literary and
condemn the gays as a wickedness against nature
Most of us accept there are people born with
feelings that are not the standard way of love
We have no right to judge them for the accident
birth, no more than the queers, demand they
are the regular ones and the rest of us insane
that some of us will not break bread with them.

The red necktie

He woke on the sofa, fully dressed
vaguely remembered an argument with a woman
He took a shower, made coffee
turned on the radio that told of a woman strangled
by a red necktie.
He paled under his fake tan; his tie was red, lost in
a brawl in a bar, did he? No, he was a friendly sort
he liked to think of himself, surely not…!
What to do now? Call the police and confess
To a crime, he could not remember having committed?
He looked out of the window into an empty street
Sunday morning, people were still sleeping
or perhaps the street had been cleared so that they could
arrest him without using force?
Now, he needed a drink, opened the drink cabinet
and there was his tie knotted on the solid neck
of whisky bottle

What lays ahead

I have for some time not eaten boiled cabbage
it is not of the slightest importance if not boiled
with shoulder ham.

On the roadway, a shop sells eggs and teaches you
how to make scrambled eggs a change from eating
the endless pizza.

Besides the egg shop, a driving school endlessly
telling would-be drivers: you drive the car, the car
is not driving you.

This mantra is forgotten as soon as new drives
hit the motorway, an ancient hatred is given free rein
to the disgrace suffered when learning how to drive.

What lays ahead

I have for some time not eaten boiled cabbage
it is not of the slightest importance if not boiled
with shoulder ham.

On the roadway, a shop sells eggs and teaches you
how to make scrambled eggs a change from eating
the endless pizza.

Besides the egg shop, a driving school endlessly
telling would-be drivers: you drive the car, the car
is not driving you.

This mantra is forgotten as soon as new drives
hit the motorway, an ancient hatred is given free rein
to the disgrace suffered when learning how to drive.

How to Become a Fascist

Clan thinking and group thinking are always dangerous
Our loyalty to the group we belong to betrays us
Waving of flags makes us think we have the right on our side
We are blind to the downside of this certainty
We stop considering an alternative, our narrowness
Makes us think other people suffering is their fault
For not following our path of righteousness
When outsiders reject our way, we react with fury
We will, in the name of freedom (ours) and slay
Any opponent as an enemy of our holly values
we say we must protect ourselves against this villainy
our rationale is unconscious fascism.

The onanist

I know of a man when following a nature trail
saw a sampling of a tree that looked neglected
dropped his semen on the tree in compassion
Years later, he visited, the sampling now a tree
which he sentimentally called my son and built
A fence around it and cut the branches of trees
that touched his son.
It was a lonely tree with an aristocratic look
There it stood posh among the forest's trees
where squirrels had fun, so sad, so gloomy
On a stormy night, his son fell, no one heard
the sound; the man said, my son, my son, why
didn't I let you grow like a forest tree should.

A nuclear war wished for

There is among the youth of the West an ingrained boredom
a hidden wish to swipe away from the old world they live in
they can't see for mist on windows and need to clear the view
the dream of an exploding world where they will be survivors.
If a few survive. they will soon wish they hadn't the destruction
will be complete, save from cockroaches and perhaps
a few ulcerated dogs will die of starvation.
As for the rich, in their bunkers, will turn against one another
eat their children and finally open the door to an empty world
Their scream for mercy to an absent god will echo forever.

In the News Today

How much liquid does a soldier's water bottle contain?
Do we need to know, or do we want to know? Probably not
Whatever it is, the secret will be exposed when a young
man is handed the keys to the safe.
90 % of secrets are trivial, filling up electronic air-ways
The 10% tells us of the skullduggery leaders are up to
Self-important, but dangerous fools they are.
What shocked me in the news this morning was what
happened in Texas, when 18000 cows were killed in
a fire; how was this tragedy possible?
Are the milking cows kept indoors in a gigantic barn
while the grass grows on the prairies? But I think
This is animal cruelty on a massive scale
should we drink milk from animals to avoid this
catastrophe from happening? I fear this will occur again
we are the destroyers of a beautiful planet that have
room for all living beings.

fidelity

The soil in the field where the vines are planted is rusty red
the mould in my hand is moist, and I feel the living pulsing wow
that will never turn stale but keep producing pleasure and
to make happiness.

To be a part of nature, unlike the religious people who think
they are in charge of fauna and fauna, and nature, should bend
to their demands, a detrimental to our goodness
There are times when in a dreamy mood and wish I could see.

A higher power deity to come down and sort the mess we are
today, we are fallible; God lost his heart in sorrow, became
a rain cloud that hovers around, ready to dampen a moment
of sunlight and contentment.

Saturday afternoon

The wind blew hard this afternoon in Cascais
whirls of dry soil, the dust, smarted eyes
Not much fun walking around doing nothing
looking into shop windows of expensive dresses
A barber shop was still open, and a barber with
scissors in his hand looked haughty, challenging
me to enter, oh, no, my man, my wife cuts my hair
I hate having a haircut, a few strands of hair left
on my scalp, may not grow back.
Horses turn their back to the wind, and I had to
face the blast going home.
I sat on the terrace, looking at the sea that
was greenish today; I don't look at the ocean
often having seen the sea until tedium
while waiting for the potatoes to boil.
But I do remember the Caribbean Sea, with
a dulcet smile.

Long is the morning

Why are you gazing into a blank future, seeing nothing
Why are you so tired today not sleeping well, still need
more sleep; the body aches like it needs more rest;
were your dreams haunted?
Old man, are you sitting there, not getting up
waiting for the surge of vitality to enter your ruined frame
thinking you are but one step from death.
Primordial man, stop dreaming of your youth when
life was easy since being young was hard, and had
many tabus and awkwardness happened many times
It is dishonest to forget the many hellish things you
Survived, when in the deepest despair, thought
of ending your life
Get up! Ancient man, ignore the pain and aches, you
are a winner in life's stakes, show you're your mettle
once more, even if you have to fake it.

Sunday forenoon and a dog

The Sunday market in the town
is slowing down, time for lunch
Chatty people leave
What is left is dust
Torn wrapping paper
And a dead dog near the bins
The cur's snout is open, showing white teeth
The roof of the dog's muzzle
is pink with brown spots
it must have been a young dog.
Silence.

The enemy within

There has been a war up North but after some times
the occupying forces surrendered and took the train
back where they came from.
Newspapers and magazines were (for a while) free
of censors, and horrific stories and pictures emerged
which the boy didn't grasp and soon forgot.
75 years later, the boy, now an old man laid up in
a hospital ward gazing at a white wall, remembered
the horrific photos he had seen.
Pictures of sexual deviations, torture and murder
not committed by the foreign occupier but by
opportunists who thrive in the shadow of wars
Sociopaths for whom other lives do not matter
to enrich themselves and indulge in obscene sex
that cumulate in strangling their unlucky victims.
Sociopathy is not an illness, is for them normal
as they are not humans and therefore lack humanity
love is for them, feelings of scant importance.
They, the sociopaths, are well-educated people
found in politics, the clerics, armed forces and
business, where they can exercise power over others
The war in Ukraine is a good example they are
pumping in weapons and refusing any peace negotiation
to the extent of risking a nuclear Armageddon.

The fame machines

He found his old type-writer in the basement
took it up, tried to clean the type face
On a day he felt like a writer dreaming of fame
hammering out a novel in a cloud of cigarette
smoke and whisky at his side
The aber was, he didn't smoke and had no tolerance
for whisky; when he did drink, he always ended up
drinking the whole bottle
relaying on his friends in the A. A to come and
take him to a meeting.
He recently bought a computer, a big, black thing
he hardly knew how to handle, nevertheless it was
going to make him instantly famous
No words came
In the evening, nervous of drinking too much coffee
he wrote a poem "the red necktie."

The truth moment

Memories are broken mirrors on
which the sun shines
the enduring illusion
sprinkled with the rest of my childhood
The dreamy imagined what ensued
or was at the time
kismet no one could foresee
Past and future pain him; he shall not see his orchard
no pictures exist he, fell off his bike
no longer a hero on a scooter
What he knows is inaccessible happiness
like a fairytale
another illusion killed stone dead.
His banalities were like trying on a great man's shoes

The Islanders

On this naked treeless island
women leave in droves
lured by TV ads, hairdresser's
and shopping spree.
Men, remains, turning to each other
In the jacuzzi, when in need
They, the men, are rich here
Flocks of sheep
need to be sheared and slaughtered
The island if famous
for its lean meat
On the mainland they would be
Nobodies, in the maelstrom
Of unemployment
After all, it is far better to be
Royals then a subjects.

The farewell

The family visitors from the town
was standing by the roadway
waiting for the bus
taking them back into the town
He, the boy, came from
although the boy liked staying
at the farm, his heart belonged
with those leaving.
He heard the bus approach and stop
He was hiding behind a stone-fence
No, he wasn't going to cry
They called his name
but only when the bus left
did he get up and waved

senses

it is about now knowing what you know except in certain circumstances
when fractures appear; when the past and the future merge.
The authorities were looking for a sunken U-boat using underwater drones
they found many things
A brig, sunk in a storm a luminosity of a lone figure looking up and smiling
before turning into unseen dust.
A German U-boat surrendered, waving a white cloth but such was the hatred
the boat was sunk anyway
They found the sub-marine had a design flaw when diving too steep an angle
the sub could not rectify itself but kept going down.
They heard and didn't hear the scream of a young realizing he should never know
the sweetest love.
The fifth dimension is the moment when the past and the present merge and
everything is understood clearly but never spoken of

Loss of faith

We're going to a Christmas party for a large family of Edvin and Maria
a couple very much in love, so much so that they looked as if not
belonging to the family they had created.

We went there because one of the sons was mother's lover, which
I didn't know at the time, but I do remember my dislike of him for
being too friendly to my mother.

A knock on the door, a hush from the children and in came St Claus
with a jute sack full of presents; to my horror, I saw it was Maria
shocked, I realized they had told me lies.

After this, I lost my childish belief in Christianity and other
religions, is as Carl Marx said: "opium for the people. "
To live well, one has to be honest; nothing else matters.

in our corrupt times, we must stand firm against the deceitful
I'm firmly against abortions, an aversion to the easy solution
like it should be a human right! (It is not)

Having no faith in fairytales, I do what I think is right! at the time
following my human sense of what is right; no, it is not easy
but I'm free of the burden of religion.

Still, one is curious, what does Nothing means?

A Man and his shadow

Followed by his shadow the appeared huge
He was going to the supermarket for an apple
When he came out his shadow gone, this

Disturbed him greatly; he didn't know a cloud
Had passed over collecting shadows
To himself he said, without a shadow I'm dead

Fearful, he took a bite of the apple, it tasted ok
Reassured he sat on some steps and waited
The shadow didn't appear this late afternoon

The man, throwing the apple core away began
Crossing the road all by himself and was hit
By a seven-ton, speeding, red lorry.

This was the moment when the cloud released
The shadow that had nowhere to go and slanted
joined the dancing syncope.

A reflections

A creaking
Staircase
linoleum floor.
A table
In a corner
A single rose.
Memories
Need no drama
The silence.
Is crescendo
Of voices
Forever stilled.

The miss adventures

He sat in his cell that was Nordic and sober
he waited for the winners to find him guilty of sedition
as the political mood was against him.
He had been to assist the starving people, the victim
of a brutalized and fanatic red socialist system
that lacked humanity
He had been vociferous in his vehemence against
the red dictator and his gang of murderers, but alas
his warnings had been met with a shrug.
Tragedy struck, and his country was invaded by forces
who had the same view of communism as him
unwisely, he joined them.
When peace broke out, the foreign forces left
he was promptly arrested as a traitor to the state
his friend, the major, had been shot.
When his case came to court, sanity had returned
the court gave him twenty years for high treason
the press had used harsh words against him
He had committed an understandable crime
but he was unable to feel remorse as his war aims
was; he was shot dead in the basement of
the people's house.

unanswered

When the window crumbles
When windows have broken
When doors slam in the wind
When the warded goes home
When they have set you free
When it is time to murmur
When you say, is that entirely

Night in Lisbon

Once, I went to a dance hall in Lisbon
 an awful place full of desperate middle-aged women
hoping to catch a man, any man.

Ah, for the horrible colors looking putrid on the wall
Was the music supplied by a jukebox when
the accordion was too drunk to play

Scrawny women of the night sat around the dance
floor trying to look sophisticated smoking cigarettes
laughing loudly like ugly sisters

Ogling men's mid-part while showing spindly legs
meant, I think, to look enticing but only succeeded
In appearing like stick insects

Once these women had been beauties, attracted
to men in uits; many divorces later and partying
time had taken a heavy toll.

Lonely women, chasing what once was, the youth
consorting with contemptible men who feared
being alone on a night when truth

www.ingramcontent.com/pod-product-compliance
Lightning Source LLC
LaVergne TN
LVHW090043160826
845672LV00013B/627

* 9 7 8 9 3 6 3 5 4 4 2 5 3 *